W9-AWK-579

Evil Twin Publications

NEW YORK

Many thanks to family, friends, and helpers at dog shows: Ryan Bourquin, Emmy Catedral, Ella Christopherson, Alexa Forosty, Peno Goble, Colin Lacey, Jody and Nick Lacey, Alex Lesy, Robert Massman, Michael Quevedo, Annick Shen and Matt Weingarden, and a very special thanks to Luke Hoverman.

This book could not have been made without the help and generosity of the owners who allowed their pets to be photographed.

Thanks to Michelle Barlak and Andrea Jordan Lane and the American Kennel Club.

ON THE COVER:

KOMONDOR	BOSTON	VIZSLA	ENGLISH	PARSON	AFGHAN	SHIH TZU	CURLY-COATED
"Quincy"	TERRIER	"Lucy"	SPRINGER	RUSSELL	HOUND	"Faith"	RETRIEVER
	"Pepper"		SPANIEL	TERRIER	"Doobie"		"Milo"
			"Trinity"	"Martha"			

Published by:

Evil Twin Publications

PO Box 2, Livingston Manor, New York 12758

eviltwinpublications.com

In association with:
D.A.P./Distributed Art Publisher
155 Avenue of the Americas, 2nd Floor
New York, New York 10013-1507

d·a·p

artbook.com

ISBN 978-0-9763355-3-5
First edition printed September 2010.

SHOW DOGS

A PHOTOGRAPHIC BREED GUIDE

BY KATE LACEY

BORDER TERRIER "Merlin"

PUBLISHER'S PREFACE

The American Kennel Club recognizes over 160 breeds of dogs in 7 categories: Hound, Working, Sporting, Non-sporting, Terrier, Toy and Herding. Thousands of Americans own purebred show dogs, and local kennel clubs host events year round at which judges evaluate how closely individual dogs conform to breed standards. Dogs are groomed to exact specifications by owners and professional handlers, ribbons and trophies are bestowed, and points are accumulated. The ultimate event in a show dog's life is Westminster—held in New York every year since 1877—which attracts hordes of visitors and an international media bonanza.

In 2005 *Life* magazine assigned photographer Kate Lacey to cover Westminster. She decided that instead of walking around Madison Square Garden documenting the scene, she would rig up a seamless backdrop to make elegant portraits, much as Richard Avedon once captured glamorous celebrities. Though partial to poodle-mutt mixes herself, on this assignment Kate became entranced by show dogs. Their exquisite grooming and acclimatization to attention made them ready subjects. And within the circumscribed limits of each breed's conformity, Kate found in every dog she met a thrilling depth of individuality—her lucid portraits shimmer with personality. After the assignment ended, she continued traveling to dog shows in a quest to photograph every one of the AKC-recognized breeds.

Some of the dogs in this book are veterans of years of shows and some are just puppies; but their achievements in the ring are not the point here. Accompanying the portraits are the nicknames they're called by the people who love them, not their official championship names, which convey their titles and lineage. The dogs in this book are like supermodels off duty, showing us a personal side in a candid moment. What we love about these dogs is not their fancy parentage and titles, but exactly what we love about every dog in our lives: their quirky and wonderful dogginess.

Stacy Wakefield, Evil Twin Publications

SPORTING DOGS

GERMAN WIREHAIRED POINTER
"Tori"

CLUMBER SPANIEL
"Jay Jay"

GOLDEN RETRIEVER
"Roy"

SPINONE ITALIANO
"Renzo"

LABRADOR RETRIEVER
"Lucy"

VIZSLA "Lucy"

FLAT-COATED RETRIEVER
"Kallie"

CHESAPEAKE BAY RETRIEVER
"Naussica"

GERMAN SHORTHAIRED POINTER
"Ceilidh"

WEIMARANER
"Stewie"

PARTI-COLOR COCKER SPANIEL
"Diva"

COCKER SPANIEL, A.S.C.O.B.
"Justice"

BLACK COCKER SPANIEL
"Miracle"

BRITTANY
"Wade"

NOVA SCOTIA DUCK TOLLING RETRIEVER
"Birdie"

GORDON SETTER
"Max"

FIELD SPANIEL
"Burke"

IRISH SETTER
"Timothy"

SUSSEX SPANIEL
"Jordin"

HOUNDS

LONGHAIRED DACHSHUND
"Bailey"

WIREHAIRED DACHSHUND "Gunther"

BASSET HOUND
"Sadie"

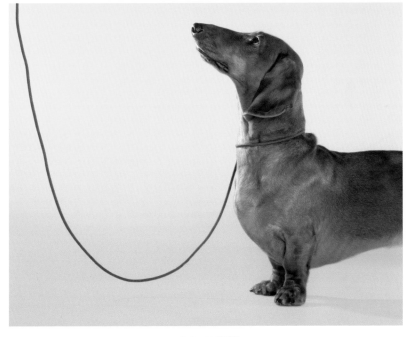

SMOOTH DACHSHUND
"Dieter"

IRISH WOLFHOUND "Winnie"

SCOTTISH DEERHOUND
"Jynx"

OTTERHOUND
"Morgan"

AFGHAN HOUND
"Maxine"

BORZOI
"Kotov"

SALUKI, FEATHERED
"Rena"

SALUKI, SMOOTH-COATED
"BJ"

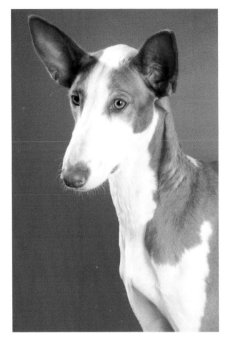

IBIZAN HOUND
"Windy"

BASENJI
"Pilot"

PHARAOH HOUND
"Bek"

GREYHOUND
"Violet"

13-INCH BEAGLE
"Reba"

HARRIER
"Merlin"

15-INCH BEAGLE
"Nicholas"

AMERICAN FOXHOUND
"Joker"

PLOTT
"Capone"

BLACK AND TAN COONHOUND
"Maserati"

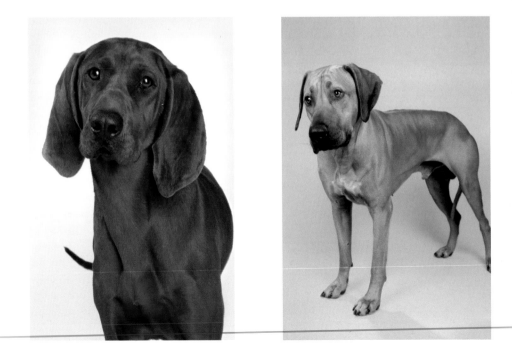

REDBONE COONHOUND
"Delbert"

RHODESIAN RIDGEBACK
"Blu"

WORKING
DOGS

NEWFOUNDLAND
"Chuck"

ROTTWEILER "Cal"

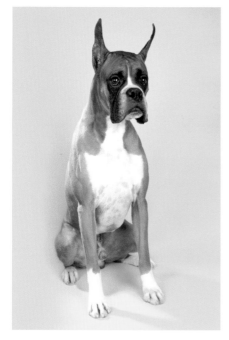

BOXER
"Derek"

GERMAN PINSCHER
"Rommel"

DOBERMAN PINSCHER
"Sonador"

GREAT DANE
"Carrie"

MASTIFF
"Morgan Rose"

SAINT BERNARD
"Mickey"

NEAPOLITAN MASTIFF
"Moses"

BULLMASTIFF
"Fancy"

STANDARD SCHNAUZER "Abbey"

BERNESE MOUNTAIN DOG
"Gracie Lu"

GREATER SWISS MOUNTAIN DOG
"Tanner"

BLACK RUSSIAN TERRIER
"Zack"

CANE CORSO
"Rambo"

SIBERIAN HUSKY "Cookie"

SAMOYED
"Vinnie"

ALASKAN MALAMUTE
"Tackle"

GREAT PYRENEES
"Estée"

LEONBERGER
"Furion"

AKITA
"Edge"

ANATOLIAN SHEPHERD DOG
"Mulch"

TERRIERS

BORDER TERRIER
"Tilda"

NORWICH TERRIER
"Shooter"

NORFOLK TERRIER
"Holly"

GLEN OF IMAAL TERRIER
"Curry"

CESKY TERRIER
"Katrina"

LAKELAND TERRIER
"Sweet Pea"

CAIRN TERRIER
"Tara"

BEDLINGTON TERRIER
"Wilton"

WEST HIGHLAND WHITE TERRIER
"Gator"

AIREDALE TERRIER
"Tess"

KERRY BLUE TERRIER
"Georgie Girl"

DANDIE DINMONT TERRIER
"Meg"

IRISH TERRIER
"Thatcher"

MINIATURE SCHNAUZER
"Mark"

WIRE FOX TERRIER
"Frenzy"

STAFFORDSHIRE BULL TERRIER
"Max"

MINIATURE BULL TERRIER
"Stache"

AMERICAN STAFFORDSHIRE TERRIER "Matty"

MANCHESTER TERRIER
"Jiggy" and "G.G."

PARSON RUSSELL TERRIER
"Martha"

SMOOTH FOX TERRIER
"Phoebe"

TOY BREEDS

TOY POODLE
"Suzie"

SHIH TZU "Faith"

HAVANESE
"Maddy"

MALTESE
"Snorrer"

ENGLISH TOY SPANIEL
"Berry"

PEKINGESE
"Danny Boy"

PUG
"Ringo"

PAPILLON
"BJ"

LONG-COATED CHIHUAHUA "Fanny"

SMOOTH-COATED CHIHUAHUA
"Walli"

CHINESE CRESTED
"Pearl"

POMERANIAN "Cee Cee"

AFFENPINSCHER
"Bailey"

CAVALIER KING CHARLES SPANIEL
"Emerson"

JAPANESE CHIN
"Yoshi"

TOY FOX TERRIER
"Booker"

ITALIAN GREYHOUND
"Claire"

MINIATURE PINSCHER
"Cowboy" and "Hattie"

BRUSSELS GRIFFON
"Newton"

YORKSHIRE TERRIER
"Tyler"

THE NON-SPORTING GROUP

BOSTON TERRIER
"Pepper"

KEESHOND
"Hammer"

SHIBA INU
"Kodi"

AMERICAN ESKIMO DOG
"Kodie"

SCHIPPERKE
"Johnny"

TIBETAN SPANIEL
"Chomo"

CHINESE SHAR-PEI
"Cruise"

LÖWCHEN
"Ruffio"

BICHON FRISE
"Sugar Bear"

HERDING DOGS

GERMAN SHEPHERD DOG
"Bullet"

NORWEGIAN BUHUND
"Lola"

AUSTRALIAN CATTLE DOG
"Rags"

BEAUCERON
"Ozzie"

BELGIAN MALINOIS
"Brutus"

ROUGH COLLIE
"Emma"

BORDER COLLIE
"Zoe"

SMOOTH COLLIE
"Rip"

BELGIAN SHEEPDOG
"Waylan"

CARDIGAN WELSH CORGI
"Freddy"

PULI
"Bo"

AUSTRALIAN SHEPHERD
"Samson"

CANAAN DOG
"Ricky"

OLD ENGLISH SHEEPDOG
"Miles"

BRIARD
"Quiere"

ABOUT THE AUTHOR

Kate Lacey is a photographer who has worked on assignment for dozens of publications including *Artforum*, *Bust*, *InStyle*, *Life*, *Make*, *Nylon*, *People*, *ReadyMade*, and the *New York Times*. Kate studied photography at Sarah Lawrence College and lives in Brooklyn. This is her first book.

Kate is pictured above with her best-in-show, Snack.

Breed	No.	Breed	No.	Breed	No.
Affenpinscher	79	Borzoi	30	Dachshund, Smooth	27
Afghan Hound	30	Boston Terrier	84	Dachshund, Wirehaired	26
Airedale Terrier	62	Bouvier des Flandres	111	Dalmatian	89
Akita	53	Boxer	43	Dandie Dinmont Terrier	62
Alaskan Malamute	51	Briard	108	Doberman Pinscher	43
American Eskimo Dog	88	Brittany	19	Dogue de Bordeaux	44
American Foxhound	37	Brussels Griffon	82	English Cocker Spaniel	17
American Staffordshire Terrier	68	Bull Terrier	66	English Setter	10
Anatolian Shepherd Dog	53	Bull Terrier, Miniature	67	English Springer Spaniel	20
Australian Cattle Dog	100	Bulldog	93	English Toy Spaniel	74
Australian Shepherd	108	Bullmastiff	45	Entlebucher Mountain Dog	106
Australian Terrier	57	Cairn Terrier	59	Field Spaniel	21
Basenji	32	Canaan Dog	108	Flat-Coated Retriever	14
Basset Hound	27	Cane Corso	49	Fox Terrier, Smooth	69
Beagle, 13-Inch	37	Cavalier King Charles Spaniel	79	Fox Terrier, Wire	65
Beagle, 15-Inch	37	Cesky Terrier	59	French Bulldog	92
Bearded Collie	110	Chesapeake Bay Retriever	14	German Pinscher	43
Beauceron	100	Chihuahua, Long-Coated	76	German Shepherd Dog	98
Bedlington Terrier	60	Chihuahua, Smooth-Coated	77	German Shorthaired Pointer	14
Belgian Malinois	100	Chinese Crested	77	German Wirehaired Pointer	8
Belgian Sheepdog	103	Chinese Shar-Pei	90	Glen of Imaal Terrier	59
Belgian Tervuren	101	Chow Chow	96	Golden Retriever	11
Bernese Mountain Dog	49	Clumber Spaniel	11	Gordon Setter	21
Bichon Frise	95	Cocker Spaniel, A.S.C.O.B.	16	Great Dane	43
Black and Tan Coonhound	38	Cocker Spaniel, Black	16	Great Pyrenees	53
Black Russian Terrier	49	Cocker Spaniel, Parti-Color	16	Greater Swiss Mountain Dog	49
Bloodhound	36	Collie, Rough	103	Greyhound	32
Bluetick Coonhound	39	Collie, Smooth	103	Harrier	37
Border Collie	103	Curly-Coated Retriever	15	Havanese	73
Border Terrier	54	Dachshund, Longhaired	24	Herding Dogs	98